Short u and Long u

Play
a Game

written by Jane Belk Moncure
illustrated by Helen Endres

THE CHILD'S WORLD

MANKATO, MN 56001

Library of Congress Cataloging in Publication Data

Moncure, Jane Belk.
  Short "u" and Long "u" play a game.

  (Play with vowel sounds)
  SUMMARY: Introduces the long and short "u"
sounds.
  1. English language—Vowels—Juvenile literature.
[1. English language—Vowels]   I. Endres, Helen.
II. Title.   III. Series.
PE1157.M65   428'.1   79-10306
ISBN 0-89565-093-2 -1991 Edition

Short u and Long u

Play
a Game

This is  . He has a special sound.

Umbrella begins with his  sound

So does **up**.

Open up the umbrella!

This is . She has a different sound.

Unicorn begins with her  sound.

So does ukulele.

Can you hear the [short U] and the [Long U] sounds?

umbrella

up

One day,  said, "Let's play a game.

I will look for my sound in words. And

ukulele

unicorn

you can look for your sound in words.

We'll see who can find the most words.''

 found underclothes,

lots of underclothes

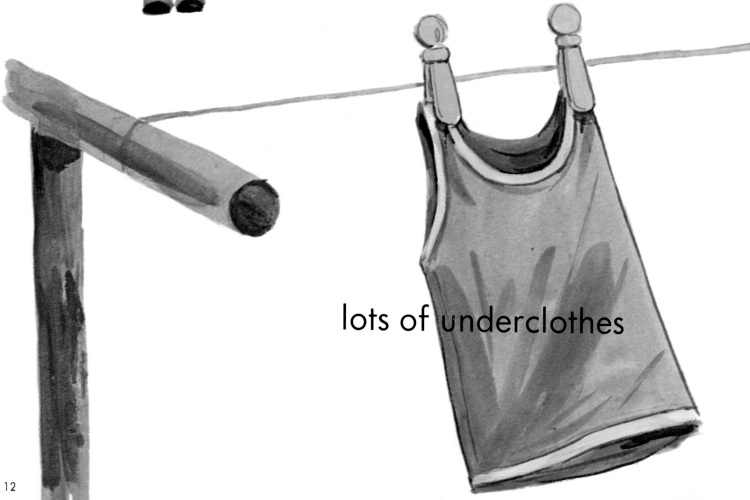

on a clothesline.

"I will win," he said.

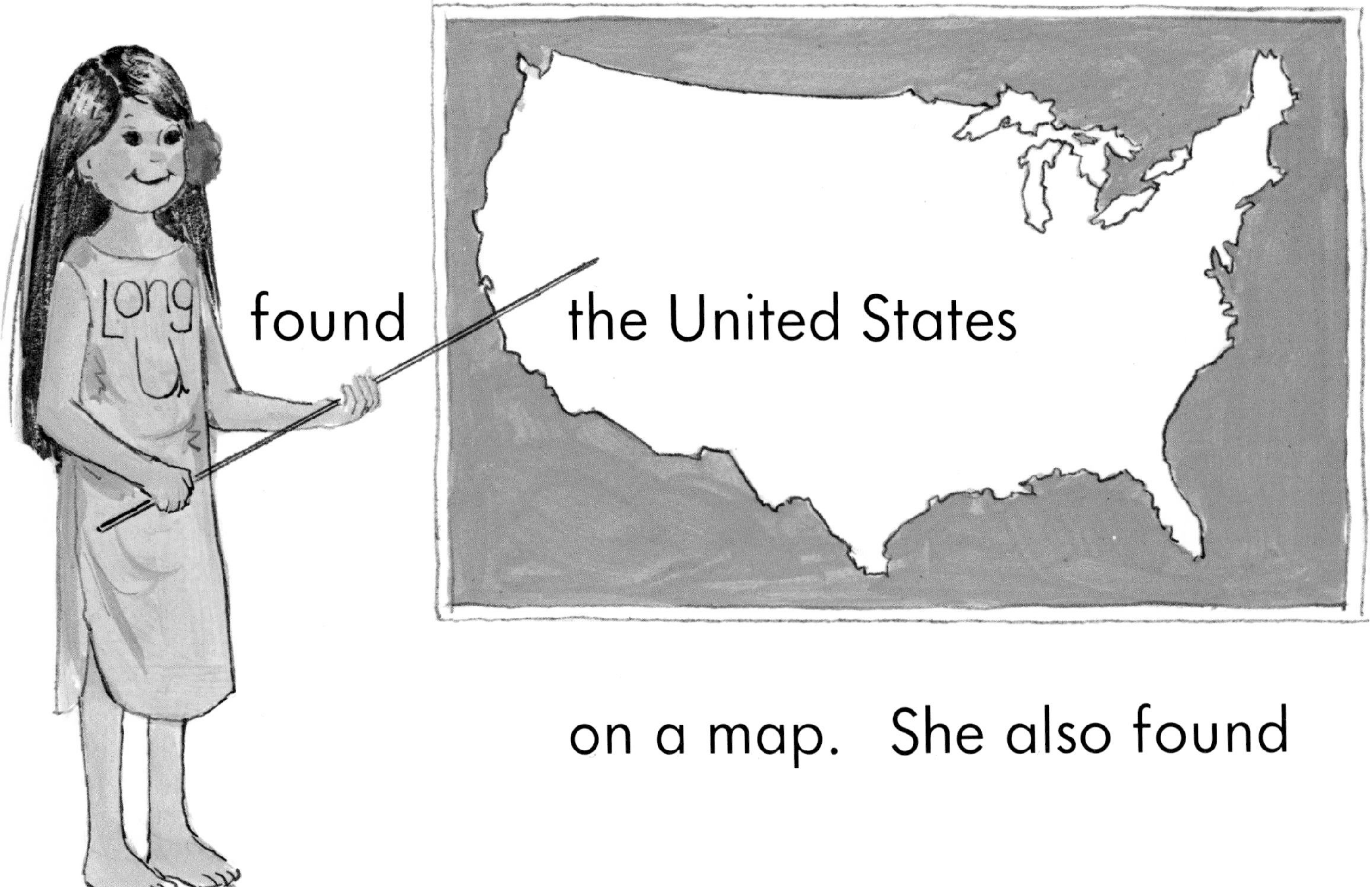

found   the United States

on a map.   She also found

uniforms, lots of uniforms.

"I will win," she said.

unicorn

uniforms

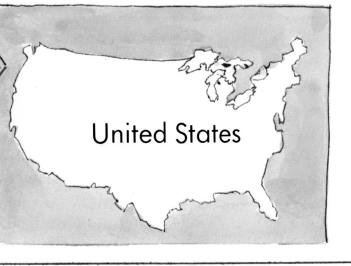
United States

ukulele

counted. "I win," she said. "I have the most words."

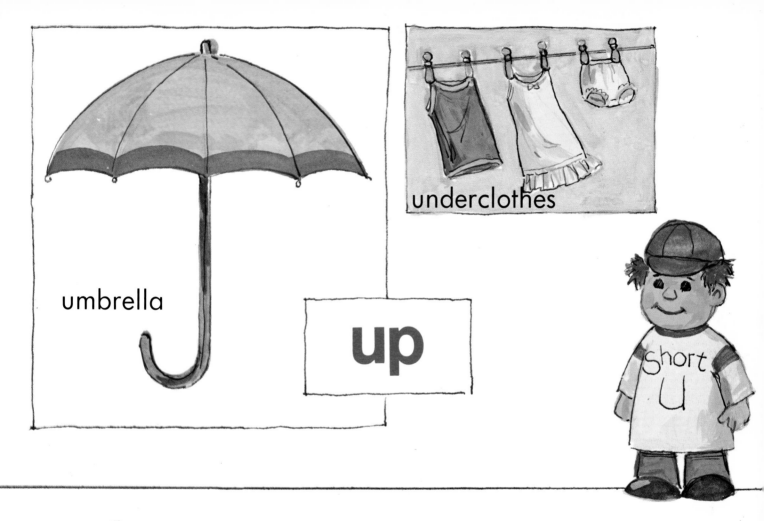

umbrella

up

underclothes

 counted. "No! No! No!" he said.

17

''I will use my eyes

and ears.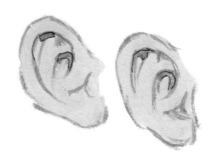

My sound hides in words. I will find words with my sound in the middle of them.''

found a

duck in a

mud puddle.

Then  found a dump truck

stuck in the mud!

He also found the sun,

buttercups,

a butterfly,

and pups,

pups,

pups!

"Now I win!" said .

 said "No! No! No!"

"I will use my eyes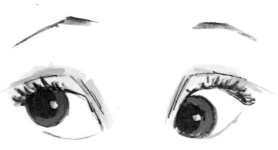

and my ears.

My sound hides in words too. I will find
words with my sound in the middle of them."

found two mules,

a cucumber,

and a cupid.

"Now I win!" said .

underclothes

umbrella

dump truck

sun

up

butterfly

duck

pups

Short U

buttercup

mud puddle

Can you tell

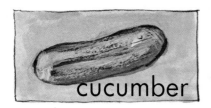
cucumber

cupid

ukulele

unicorn

mule

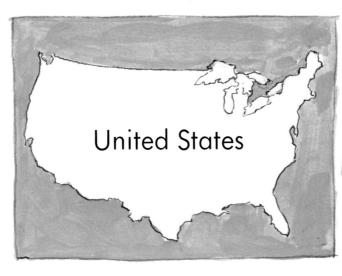
United States

who won?

Can you read more words with ?

bus

puppet

gum

YUM GUM

skunk

bunny

bubbles

brush

bucket

28

Can you read more words with 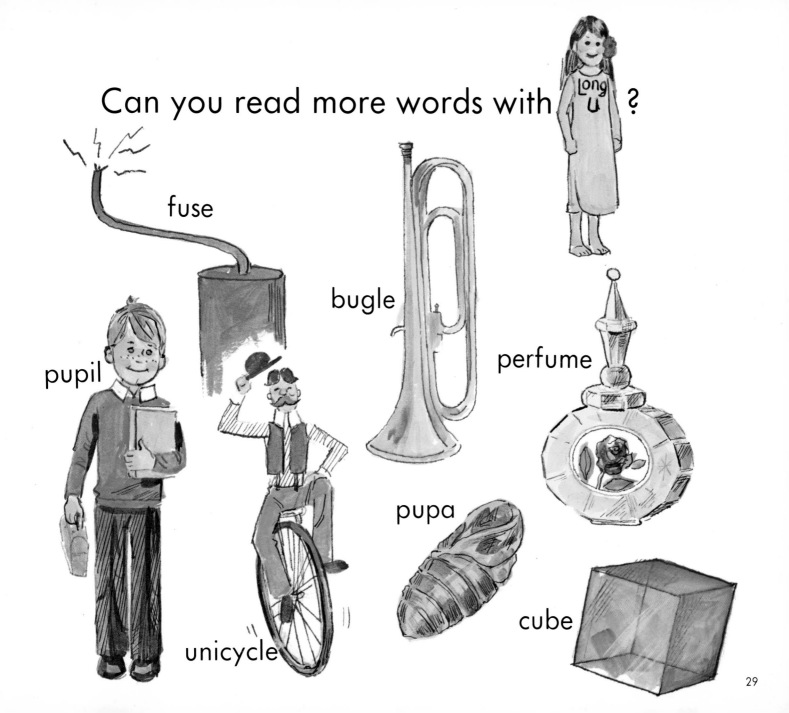 ?

fuse

pupil

bugle

perfume

unicycle

pupa

cube

Now you make up a game!